GW01459848

The WAQ-WAQ TREE
and other poems

The WAQ-WAQ TREE

and other poems

Patricia Tyrrell

SixForty Press

First published in 2006 by SixForty Press
17 Century Court, Porth, Newquay, Cornwall TR7 3JP.

A catalogue record for this book is available from the British Library

ISBN   -0-9537947-2-5

Designed and typeset by Authority Publishing
Set in Garamond and Myriad Pro

Printed in the UK by T J International Ltd, Padstow, Cornwall.

For Carolyn and Terry

Patricia Tyrrell is an Anglo-American who now lives in Cornwall. Collections of her poems have previously appeared from Flarestack Publishing and Pikestaff Press. She has also written three novels: *Into the Promised Land* (runner-up for the 2001 Sagittarius Prize), *The Bones in the Womb* (shortlisted for the 2003 Encore Award and republished as *The Reckoning*) and *Grandmother Wolf*.

Acknowledgements Most of these poems have appeared before, either as prizewinning entries in competition anthologies or in *Human is Not Enough* (Flarestack Publishing, 1997) or *Prime Numbers* (Pikestaff Press, 2003) or in one or other of the following: *Cadenza, Chillout, Envoi, The Interpreter's House, Magma, The North, Obsessed with Pipework, Other Poetry, Poetry News, Poetry Review, Poetry Nottingham International, The Rialto, Sepia, She, Stand, Staple, Tabla Book of New Verse, Tears in the Fence, The Times, The Writer* (USA), *Treasure Hunting, Writers' News*. Grateful thanks are due to the editors of those publications.

CONTENTS

Light Verse

Early Poems

The WAQ-WAQ TREE

The Waq-Waq Tree

an ancient myth

Magnificently, in a dream,
the parrot stalked my shoulder.
He and I stood on the edge of the world
and stared together at the Waq-Waq tree
which sprouts human souls instead of leaves.
I shall not soon forget the parrot.

As he reminded me at the time (while absently
nibbling my left ear) he was once a vulture
but has tidily metamorphosized. Humans
don't enjoy vultures murmuring to them
near the edge of the world. This parrot is pragmatic.

The Waq-Waq shifted its sombre leaves at us.
A soul fell here, fell there, quite disregarded
except by us. The parrot said,
'Is there no one to gather these souls up
and transport them?' No one appeared,
only the Waq-Waq muttered in the desert

there at the edge of time, where all things crash
as if they've run into a wall. The parrot said,
'It's a crying shame,' and I retorted,
'What would you do?' So he, embarrassed,
said, 'Nothing. We're ill-equipped.' We turned away
and heard the Waq-Waq drop those unregarded leaves
behind us.

Old Foreign Films

Sword-warriors a millimetre thick,
mourners like bellied pigs half soaked with brine
or one lean solitary woman sheathed in black,
the Gauloise smoke spiralling ragged O's,
the leisurely allusive glass of wine,

the horizon's ruined tree, the brief embrace
avid yet sombre, and the gleam of knife
or clear shard, carnival or clown,
the stolen bicycle, the grin of circus child:
I learned to breathe from these, I learned my life.

Donkey and saint, whore and young sadist, all
in one great pulsing circle roughly fused,
shout through the decades so that still each day,
arriving, flickers like an ancient nitrate film,
decay-splotched but ironic, glad, amused.

Baby in Church

A baby thumps his woman with dictator fists,
kills the priest's papery drone; my concentration swerves,
hooked by the Chandleresque frown a half-inch wide.

Amid his roars (Ferrari cutting all curves,
super-sure the world will step aside)
his travelling gaze finds me, new variable

in his near circle. His astounded eyes
pull me with him to jump on carousels –
fragilely spinning, painted, mythical.

Does his calm mother glimpse those carousels,
or does (I plead) childbearing blur acuteness?
(Now I beg coins to compensate us barrens).

Nothing can shift the fact that he's her son
(milk-smell drips from her and the loins sag used)
but if my wish could tug enough, he'd leap
to spin in my belly for always. O he would.

Argument

Pause after argument. Then,
'Did you know,' I say,
'the heart is the body's toughest muscle?
Striated, dense as railroad ties,
as interwoven metal hammocks;
this is anatomic fact.
Had you realised how tough the heart is?'

And both of us smile at this.
Reluctant, shocked, we smile.

The Body's Trace Elements

'Here's gold,' as fraying maps proclaim.
I've mined in you without noticing those elements
quiet as icons in the mystery of your flesh.

What have we to do with grey-sheened zinc,
magnesium flare, copper skillet,
the salt lash of the sea,
the wince of chlorinated public baths,
a rusting iron rod,
volcano's yellow-sulphur calyx,
the painter's cobalt lure,
steel-tough molybdenum,
hint of manganese –
and the gold in us, the gold?

I could sell you tomorrow
or you me, in any commodity market
for roughly two-pounds-fifty sterling
based on the price of minerals that day.

Morning arrives like scales to calculate us.
You're first up. Where you've lain
warmth generated by our double chemistries
teases, insinuates, like an explaining,
not fool's-gold heat but the rare metal's.
I turn my lips to the shaped hollow
while, two rooms off, your singing
structures our complex new experiment.

Obsessive

To the washbasin
full of grief
to the mirror
to the wall.

To the washbasin knotting your fingers
contaminated by absent minutes,
to the mirror to check the face's details,
to the blind consoling wall.

To the washbasin in which a hair
(of what wild origin?) alphabets itself,
to the mirror where the eyes
traumatised lurch for the wall.

To the washbasin where constant scrubbing
aches your hands like a murderer who loves them,
to the mirror to survey your grovelling snout,
to the wall. Hummingbird, hummingbird

image of God, how you strain
into this sinewed compulsion:
run to washbasin, mirror, wall,
washbasin...

Delusional

There are worse fears, no doubt,
than believing you're a glass piano
about to be played by an incompetent
jangler in the mad king's castle

between dungeon and eagles. The jangler
has nails which scrape defensively
and because you're transparent his feet,
oozing and sticking, climb visibly

up the ladder inside you. You're frantic
with hammers and felts, can't consider the music
as itself, as existing like water
or sorrow or lace; can only cry

mutely between the drummings
of the compulsive chords.

      She tells me all this
and I nod, murmur soothing.

She says her frenetics remind her
of a Marx Brothers movie; she turns
her tragedy sides-to-middle,
shakes it, has to laugh

until rain on the window
returns her to turrets and arpeggios.
There are, no doubt, worse fears. But you or I
could we bear to inhabit this one?

Headline

'Who is the famous rock star with six toes?'
asks a tabloid under the gibbous moon and I realise
another huge area of knowledge is walled from me.
All I can connect with is Hemingway's cats
at his Key West typewriter, creating the ultimate Hemingway
using six toes on each foot, a vertiginous link
to the era of Gatsby and of Papa writing under the palmettos,
banging away, clattering; Papa with wives and genius
and bitchiness enough for an army. Papa inside whom
lived bones resembling voodoo, plus the thirst of an astronaut
intoxicated on gravity-freedom but ageing rapidly,
as we all do, in space. Papa who would surely have met
and would recognise, dismember, immortalise this rock star.

Mr. Stokes Jumping off a Brooklyn Wall,

October 14, 1886

Nothing is known of Mr. Stokes except this photo,
his long Abe Lincoln body
toying midair as if time were a jewelled fobwatch
he could pull from his pocket and stop.

Kids and teenagers – other subjects
of the Fort Greene photographer –
jumped awkwardly, they straddled space
like jumping into mash. But Mr. Stokes

(black suit, the fashionable inch of cuff,
silver-topped cane and derby,
lean muscled thighs) rises above his plinth
a totem thundergod, icon hurled free,

dramatic fragment, mute
as some Pompeiian worker's carve;
his cane traces the cumuli jaunty as if
lightning strikes upward and he leaps alongside.

Neat loins and composed torso, he soars
over the Civil War cannon, against the spires
and scrubby trees of the city where yesterday
on broken sidewalks I saw a T-shirt youth

wearing the message FUCT. Fucked, fact, fixed, fetched,
fraught, fierily frazzled,
frozen, fooling, flipped. The years dissolve.
What was Mr. Stokes' relationship

to those tenements, the crowded millions
who in sweatshops withered and wove?
Gone and built over, we shall never know.
Exploiter or philanthropist, he rises,

the cause of his great happiness long buried
in the leaping sepia air; gladly preoccupied
as a child with innocent sport. But mustn't our era
view with suspicion his sleek glossy joy?

After My Evening Shift

We're in bed, lights out. You're too wise
to ask how my evening went
at the hospital. But because
it wasn't bad, I tell you.
'A goodish shift, no deaths.'
The two of us lean warmly
together, muscle-tired, not sexy.
But we shall be;
between us we'll summon
the pitch-daubed canvas horse
whose urge is leaping passion,
and the child who teases it
with a twist of coloured ribbons.

Outside is winter. Hospital seasons
don't vary much except for carols
all Christmas week. Visitors cry over them;
I do too. Carols are a starter's pistol
for the next year – or lack of one.
Over some beds the walls must hide their faces.

We make love like the cakes I mix,
suitable but with a different zing.
Christmas, two astronauts and lunar module;
Valentine's Day, sticky pink hearts
with fuzzy caterpillars; Halloween,
witches on purple broomsticks, wearing robes
pale-printed like boiled eggs we customise

to Laura Ashley lisp at Easter.
That's our true lovemaking; some nights
we rein ourselves down from the ceiling,
some nights we simply gloat and fly.

I've never told you (for there's no explaining)
how in the hospital's bleak nighttime glitter
when I watch urine, blood and messier fluids
all acting wrong, I recite to myself
in silent incantation the glow-colours
of my childhood paintbox: cobalt,
rose madder, ultramarine, burnt umber.
They remind me there's a real world outside.

This evening you've read;
you tell me Henry James enjoyed a bullfight,
counted his stools when nervous, and in Rome
(some dusty Vatican courtyard)
was sure he glimpsed the Pope's petticoats airing.

Under our covers
I say, 'Dear Henry James!' and we nibble,
we fight and tease, we kiss.
I try to forget
that Henry James fell ill too, died; despite my shower
do I still reek of those atrocious stinks?
'Poor Henry James,' and I kiss you full on the lips,
our tongues explore. This night is ours –
at least this hour, this moment. Nothing's guaranteed
but the traffic outside has muted, the lamps dimmed.
Our bodies join, we rise swiftly towards the ceiling.

Backwoods Saturday Night

Heat like a laundry. Whippoorwills
and bullfrogs whose speeches jargon
the dirt road's logic. Peeling frame houses, 'Rooms'
(a gappy neon flicker). The Milky Way
leans down to take a look. Outside a bar
tall thin men lounge, the strobe lights bounce,
noise threshes to its footloose harvesting.
Greed, hope, fear, need: like pencils crammed in a jar
the lined emotions battle for expression.
Sweat, dust, lipstick and grease; then afterwards
the muttering cauldron of midnight into which,
at the cave of our pickup truck or another,
jumps love, that wild bobcat, clawing its way from the
forest.

Island in the Frozen Lake

There's no such thing as phantoms, only the brutal ghosts
of us banging each other. Winter in the high country
brings a narrowing of choice, end of evasion,
a sort of nervous peace.

When the ice settles –
ribbed like old memoires and thick as wishes,
equipped (in these roadless hills) for a car's weight –
you can walk out, like a new saviour, to the island.

Its bushes and its tall pines close about you
as if you are a secret, near forgotten
through summer's mumble of mosquito-haze
and the swoop of forktails furrowing the water
and the eagle's doorslab flight.

New diffident scratches hedge the snow like throat-clearings,
questions unanswered; the bears have stripped these bushes early,
swimming ponderous through the slush in the red days of autumn,
yet you've a feel of something walking behind you.

The hills enclose this lake like cupping the palm
of a hand sweaty with work, sweat which slowly congeals
in the circling season. Overhead a plane
(transatlantic, not greatly interested)
abstractly wonders which is earth, which ice.
Puzzle stares up at puzzle; the plane shrugs
and the pines retain you. Islands are the profoundest symbol,
basic beyond eating and loving and speech; out there

you are held like the lake-ice, are unimaginably hallowed
and surrounded. The skin which cups you stays expectant.

Winter is no time for birdcries except a rare alarm-churr,
but old pine needles rattle down like teeth
hollow upon the frozen white. Here is no wind,
no seal or fish-plop, fluid language

or polished swerve of breath. You are not shaken
within this dot which massive ice encloses,
you are statuesque, presumed important,
an Easter Island shape. The world begs you, it kneels.

Yet mockery burrows up: the thaw will find you,
will tinker with you like a boy at a wrecked car.
You must realise your danger, must recross the sodden
ice under which spiralling larvae seethe.
You have ceased to be important, you are now rejected,
a poor forked creature. Human is not enough.

Deaf

'The lot across the road
was bought by deaf folks for their summer camp.
They'll be your quietest neighbours.
Heh heh.' They never built,
just dug the usual cellarhole
then changed their plans. The land's grown up

in red oak, sumac, maple
(not sugary; we're too far south for sweetness)
and their acres buzz with noisy chatter
between leaf and bird. Very like the laughter
at an all-deaf college I once visited –
we students on assignment – and we asked

would someone speak to us in sign.
A girl gleamed at us and her fingers fluttered.
'What did she say?' so our interpreter
relayed the Ameslang: 'I-am-deaf-and-I-love-you'
whiel the other deaf students laughed in a jerky freehand way
very like leaf to bird. This flickering sun

recalls the hands that accompanied us like stacked cards
falling, falling, but sure of destination.
They've never lived here – yet the forest
has its own kind of silence, as I found
in today's mist: a golden eagle flying
with one noiseless wingbeat from ruined house to creek.

Subzero Temperatures

This week is cold enough
for my coat to walk around without me.
On the path appear
snipe and wingbeats of scarlet, of gold.
In frosts like this you suspect
that official seals on doors are being broken
out of sight but nearby;
they fall with a thin clatter
like the software of someone banished.

And words of white breath, coalesced
from invisible people,
enter the rooms which still smell
of cognac, of lily-type flowers,
bread and muscle. Now is not a reasonable day.
The cold hugs its intense habits
and refuses to give them up. Someone will master it
sooner or later, will throw the frost on its sword.
Yet I've read that a schoolboy
in the last moment of Pompeii,
amused or angry over some non-event,
wrote on the wall of a house
while the lava started to move,
'They all became silent.'

Smalltown Saleroom

'Lot 23, a merman.'
Absurd that this creature
(faked from a monkey's ribs, the skull
papier-maché on a dogfish jaw;
sinewed forelegs of lizard
and tail from common skate)
should, with the questioning poise
of its stalk-necked head, remind me
of Augustine's cry on conversion:
'My soul was sick of the man who carried it.'

After an August News Report

Heat's a fierce searching-out like any other,
a miracle by the power of demons, an arriving
without the seatbelt of a journey. By inscription
the sun burns its brown armoury
into these fields and woods. Such heat could maim;
no one has taught it sensible behaviour.

Thick bubbles bruise through the swamp, yet I'd forgotten
the rumour of a body. Murder here –
deliberate, foreplanned – is rare as ice;
a body carried from the town would surely
rise upright, clawing
wild as our hundred-foot wisterias.

The girl was never found, only her bloodstains
like starched red flowers where she'd spent the night
and disappeared next morning. My woods map
shows old foundation stones in the heart of the swamp:
stones and wisteria roots and the silt bubbles rising . . .
Whether or no, this marks the end of innocence.

Derelict House in a Cornfield

A house scraped bare to its spine;
the mood, pale light of a winter desert
even in July. You can't connect
beach parties or harvest joy with these pitted
rafters or this corner post which slants
bleak as a gunstock – and the mood
is violence, though the family moved
most likely peaceful away. To leave a house?
to let it fall? for overdue
taxes maybe; easiest to quit and run.
Or a proud indifference; the patriarch long dead
and this the bounty of the troubling youngest son
who one day up and left; what'd you expect?
isn't there always a runt who cracks from lonely pressure?

What place did he find better? (always 'he';
a woman would cling stubborn, propping, patching,
bequeath the house to kind ones on her death).
Did he flee to a sand-shack on the Outer Banks,
trembling urgently toward the next hurricane,
leaning to that, not this tired rustle
of stalks? Was this what sent him
brusquely away? that these fields, though open,
are never quiet, chatter continually
with leafage and cobs, and in the fall
argue in manic whines before they're ploughed.
And then in winter

the harsh snow-wind limps singing
its turret notes round the ditches and hills
and mutters, at these eaves, of nastier options;
was it this terror sent the mute son away?

A desert sight although the earth around it
foams green in spring. This season doesn't touch these rafters
except for termite-stir, ferocious nibbles. People need cosiness,
shelter and food; we can find, surely,
no joy at living skeletal.

Last night, in the cold nuzzling
of the hour before dawn, I dreamed into existence
a group of lakes (near Paris?), their shores bare
except for one fir-smattering. Those lakes
rested in that peculiar Gallic light
which spins itself coin-wise to the French language,
a tongue so definite that clarity
is a six-petalled flower, and étang
is the shape of the water itself,
the long thin eventfulness waiting.

France might have much to teach
America about lack of crudeness,
but some ears are formed for the rasp of the corn stalks
and the pounding by sun or snow; some eyes for this house,
its corpse perched like a familiar vulture.

Fertility Rite

The moon breaks this civilised house in pieces.
I've studied fertility rites
and most of them made reference to the moon.
Can we explain
this shattering of us, by supposing
any other cause? Plain as

a declension of ancient nouns the moon rises;
why didn't we realise
the effect of being stared at,
night after night, by a scarred whiteness
inexplicable, curtainless? And the song
(there was certainly music, though not originating

perhaps from that pallid disc)
the song was pagan, thumping
like the repeated thuds of a car stereo
which deafens and then fades into the distance, taking –
as we've now learned –
all our force with it, all our silly hopes.

Separation

I wake with your tears on my face –
you weep at someone else's complicatedness.

Sunrise is an irrelevant fire
beyond these hills, a vast incinerator.

Across me you put the phone down and we fuck again
smiling yet distant, like living next to the moon.

Did she believe you? but I won't ask; such questions
turn hollow under our scrutiny, like turning a vase

and considering its parched curve. Dear,
if you and I truly loved each other
we wouldn't be clutching here.

The Drowned Spymaster

No doubt the river lay
(like sorrow) where he least expected
and its banks overhung him

unhelpful with their timber
crooked as a casual soul.
His weekend cottage flanks mine

and my jazz of lived countries
breeds suspiciousness in me, a welter
of cockroach feet.

But the cops think no one drowned him,
he walked himself down to the creek,
slept deep and rose next morning

smudged on the waters,
a bird that would be rare in any language
now trailing a fan

of ordinary seagulls. Instruct me
how to feel about this death?
(The river slides, is oil

from a broken sump). In which
of our shared countries
did he send to the mountains for snow

to cool his lemonade
and what was the going rate?
The mahogany walls and red plush

of those old trans-Europe trains –
you smile, but there were deaths.
I decide I ought to be glad

of this bereavement; he wasn't the sort
you invite for coffee. You suspect
someone could arrive at night

to despatch him. (Of course by accident).
He who counted the towers,
now in the mortuary

his Rolex sinks into the wrist flesh
with a nearly indecent haste.
I woke once; there was a storm,

the lightning-man weaving chains.
Later I half woke; was the planeless sky
rampant with noise, an immensely labouring

unhuman sound? am I more sensitive
from his history and mine, a needle-
thrust through the pair of us

from some discarded factory?
It always astonishes me
that a derelict needle-shed

may stand harmless as any other,
its walls charred and a dead Rolex . . .
no, that was elsewhere.

I've never understood spies;
to my mind they resemble
blue swifts which hover

and sleep at the same time.
(Those shriek at midnight too).
Anyone with my past

would shiver at this death.
You who've innocently loved your country
are allowed to feel harmless –

you who have a country –
but for us mixed-Europeans
things are never so simple.

As Broadway ends
not in a dazzle but with the slow
seep of unnecessary tides, bare jetty,

boatyard of broken stilts
and watchman's splintery hut –
after that, anything

is possible. On his recent appointment
his publicity photos were taken
by men in balaclavas;

he smiled for the cameras
and the flowers on his desk were lilies
in a discreet shade of pink.

In other countries the ground freezes inward
but here cold erupts; from the soil
project inch-tall skyscrapers,

domes, mausoleums,
freeways, bus shelters. This is the first country
where I've walked upon cities of ice;

they mutter when you crush them. The spymaster surely
noticed this too.
(A healthier effect,

perhaps, than cities too confused by fear to mutter).
There's no clean explanation of the fact
that the wrecked spymaster

floating up with this morning's tide
lifted his wingless hands like blessing;
in the mental landscape we shared –

terrain of barns and falcons –
blessings are dirty work. So instruct me
how to feel about this death

and I'll refute you; there are reticences
even in folk as nearly integrated as myself.
Repeated deracination

doesn't show on the face, and yet inside
(I speak for myself only) it's quite possible
a grinning animal sits.

At the Swimming Hole

A child suddenly wearing his nakedness
    like a new and difficult garment;
eight years into this skin, he inspects it

edgily. No one is guiltless
    not people or the night-coloured grass
or small turtles who slouch

on the dirt road. The boy's no longer a centaur
    leaping in sun-puddled shallows,
he's the bird of Turkish folklore,

named but no body; he must go
    search for his real skin. Plunging repeatedly
into clear cold water, not finding.

Candlelight in the Chapel

Your absence shifts the candlelight
personal upon the wall. Outside, the gale
bangs at this roof, grunts, twitches by.
The clouds go past like hands.

These licks of smiling flame: candles are narrow,
prejudiced, waxen, but their twisting wicks
have burned for danger in more years, more corners,
than I care to recall. There were dismemberments

and other garish ploys of childish nightmare,
chilblains, intolerable beauty of frost
flowering briefly between me and the snare-world.
And, one time, huge sky-curtains

fragmented giants across the northward night,
shaking it till my science tumbled from me
and burst among those flames. 'The Northern Lights,'
my father said. Once only in a lifetime.

I have lived in all the wrong places
and hadn't met you then, my dear,
whose absence gutters these candles thinly
across the stone they move on, like inscribing.

The Smell of Apples

At midday I glimpsed the road gang sweatily trudging
with prison riflemen before and behind them,
a usual August sight; their green fatigues
blotchily reddened by the dustprints of this route.
They stared ahead except for one who glanced
to me, my pine trees, smiled. When the sun fell
the sheriff came to warn: a prisoner had escaped.
Emptily I guessed 'rapist' but no, robbery-with-assault.

After he goes I study the ring on my finger.
When you gave it me first I often looked at it
in mistake for my watch, and it told me
a different pace of happening. Since then time has become
sinewed, striated, its fibres split and spliced,
but this flight sweeps the threads apart; the robber
is the core breathing while the surrounds stop.
I could fear him, and touch, and the clocks be reluctant to warn us.

'Grab an empty life and lever into it one outlaw'
yet this absconder's likely not my noticed and is heading
nowhere (I hope) that thoughts of me would swerve him.
Freedom, the great smooth egg, how to possess it?
Blood and blunt weapons could follow. . . but I've no right
to interrogate his crimes. All night the smell of apples
in my garden, my house. A rich domestic scent
but corrupting, like danger. Unstable, poised to alter.

Tex Ritter's Guitar Strap

Engraved on the blue leather, four motifs.

Firstly, 'High Noon.'
Here in Beirut no sunbaked Western saunter, but our team
has found three Roman arches and now breaks for lunch.
We chew on pitta bread; our toecaps sift
spent bullets, shards of bone. Which sect did these workmen,
these busy dust-smoothers, fight for?
Sects tightly packed like cheeses, each one reeking.

'Rye Whiskey.'
We have watered our horses in Helicon
and in those Southern woods
where through illegal moonshine stills
the brown spring water trickles, not explaining.
Laurelled in folk memory
as holy wells are honoured in other countries,
that muttering water draws my ragged thought,
sporadic votive offering which exiles send
to the green place they've turned their backs on.
Shadbush, black oak, dogwood,
redcrested treepecker, bobcat,
inch-high pink shellflowers by the railroad every April,
remember us who have abandoned you.

'The Deck of Cards.'
Not poker here, or other Western games.
Here the cards sort like crystals under a microscope
while the inhabitants of this city play patience, patience.
Too many are dead for a full stacked-up house.

'The Book of Names.'
Insert your own for Tex's oblique scribbles.
So I proclaim
four people listed, of whom three have died.
I, the remaining quarter,
life up my gaze like a glass wall to the sun.
Walls can stay silent in many languages.

The whole of Tex Ritter's guitar strap.
Six thousand miles from me, in rural Texas,
framed in a small museum case the pure strap hangs,
its sea-blue leather shaped like a giant claw
lumbering up from the lower Gulf
all tired simplicities. It does not sing
or play, it is a weapon waiting
with a terrible innocence we wanderers cannot face.

Migration

Night triangle –
the supersonic grunt of Concorde heading home.
Half-moon. My rooftop self.

Arcane as a gust
of prepared music, thirsting
across the three of us
the small birds fly.
Skylark and finch, swallow, brown dove.

   Now on this roof
beneath their pale assured cries, I remember
the child I tutor who multiplies
numbers casual as dancing but
can't learn his mother's face.

'A Lady at the Virginals' by Vermeer

In a corridor where we can brood,
the patients and I, over lost relationships.

Her room with wall-high windows, chequered floor,
table and viol (decorative, not important),
a girl considering the keyboard of a virginals
and flatland's light and light and light.
 He views her face within arm's reach, we dimly
 in a blurred mirror; her figure is young and taut
 and the man much her elder, apparently
 feeble (leans on a stick). Her father, guardian?
 husband? (A profound unease at this).

Between the pearling brushstrokes did Vermeer
reflect on his wife, on the dazzles and shades
of being married, on their eleven children
(ranged formal to his view like pallid stones),
on his unfashionable Catholic faith?
 He couldn't paint this couple, surely,
 without getting involved; under the pure clear light
 a tension seethes and builds in both the figures.
 She never looks at him, he stares her down;
 they are disasters waiting to collide.

Or do we with our special knowledge,
our charred experience, read in too much?
can we mark a tranquil couple with our fevers
and slow the painter's hand to our agonised fumbling?

Yet one fact's real: Vermeer soon after died.
    The girl plays on; her companion watches, waits;
    outisde a man cries, 'Eels!', a cart groans by.
    Soon Vermeer's baker will knock to claim his debt –
    the brushes dry, the empty easel a-tilt
    and the light pouring, pouring.

Sequin Read

A woman made of books.
Two spines her arms and
two longer spines her legs,
strong A-4 pad her body,
smooth notepaper her face.

I opened a book tonight and
gold sequins fell out.
If I run around behind you,
pages rustling, shall I find
the masked ball in the Armoury
where these words polarised your light?

Description by Father Weston, Prisoner
of the Night of March 24, 1603

They hold me in the Tower, and tonight
all sound ebbs from the city; I had leaned
at my stone slit and watched the river traffic
till dark fell, wondering why
boats melted to the shore as if some new obedience
alchemic swerved the channel of their course.

At three a.m. – 'like a ripe apple from the tree,' the gaoler tells me.
I'd shrive him but he will have none; I tell him Rosa Solis,
instead, is a specific against fevers.
(A cheap wine, it can do no harm). He goes, muttering the name
as if it were his sovereign's legacy.

I've watched the boats sail up and down to Greenwich,
and prophesy: This summer they'll go further,
they'll all be murdered when they reach Gravesend
as plague-bearers. I am a minor prophet, burned and chipped,
honed by incarceration, am all conscience;
a sovereign's death will leave me undiluted.

Yet how did she die, bare human at the last?
Rumour says, 'Little man, princes must not be forced.'

The music of the usual dark is all dried up;
the night is stiff with stars, the shroud of Christ.
I should pray politely to Our Lady who tomorrow,
as every March, sits and admires the angel,
dutiful hears his awkward testament.

Is that a rat runs at the Lady's feet, a snake?
to what guise is my tough old sovereign fled?

I foretell further: musk will cease to stink
pretty for women's bosoms. Odours crumble,
the world annihilates itself like a great egg
that would hatch out but cannot. Does the queen-corpse
wander to pull the stars' stained folds about her?
what is a soul, this pared residual? I'm all conscience;
ask me no questions that require a gentle answer.

Something will fade which that old heretic held
in jostled reverence. Men say she knelt
at night when younger, used her prayerbook, sought
a certain god. I who can view so sharp
into some chinks of battered years to come,
why can I not foretell my death?
I'd more be disembowelled than catch plague.

I'd sooner not be disembowelled though. How still the night,
how difficult to pray when there's no noise,
no grumbled fightings, liquors, nothing but space
and a dark river and her stiffening corpse.
I'd sooner not be disembowelled, but the plague
is terrible, a hundred devils jumping on you,
all shrieking. And I shall not die of age,
have no such hope. Where is my breviary?
How still the night, how empty – and the sovereign dead.
Where then's my breviary? Gaoler, there's no light!

Man Washing Car

A thin plastic Medusa the hose fights him,
she leans against the car, her explosion of hair streaming
in the evening's slant light; her snakes all around him
gently hiss, gently. They lie down at his side
but leap up when he embraces Medusa. He's always gazing

past her, beyond, into the curved shine of the car's attention;
he knows the danger, he pretends the metal flank is all-important
yet he clutches Medusa, guides her. You would guess they're
lovers, lovers, closer than his wife in the house
who watches television and fusses because he washes his car

almost daily. You would say there's a symbiosis,
here in the gnat-pale evening, as if hose
were flesh and human plastic; they bend over the car
with a passion, a single passion. You would say
she offers herself continually, hair streaming silver from the hose,

reaching and twining; she offers and the man
continually accepts. The car is long since spotless
and there's no feel of Gorgon slain
or conquering (he still stares past her).
But with the rush of night the hair dulls pewter;

the hose twists, stiffening. The car, sardonic,
gleams in bat-tracery. He turns the taps,
wrings out his washleather, empties the bucket.
Hose now is merely hose, man merely husband.
Upon the car, garaged, a last hair dries.

An Empty Photo Booth at Night

This cube is a hammered bouquet
of formal improbable flowers;
the winds talk round it in a madman's Greek,
rattle the slots, the mirror, which await
some face who will appear and pose.

Everything shivers; the dark street's all excitement,
the lighted booth a king. The curtain plunges,
grabs at the night and wind, as in old legends
a wolf plays victim/priest. One passing walker,
caught by the curtain, stands and gapes

at the lit hole, then swerves; what has he glimpsed?
This scrappy dungeon is the bare obverse
of summer newsstands where, instead of these few props
(cigarette stubs, a small pouched rubber ring,
an edge of newspaper, a smear of gum

and the wolf-god's voice, 'You must cut off my head
now, instantly, because I've helped you,')
there spill red, gold, green, zinging books
(bizarre lifestories), magazines
to tint each different hour, and sleepingbags,

new shapes of keys; the brown proprietor –
part salesman, medic, part wise shrink –
leans with continual chat while bellied boats
grin from their moorings and the cafés shout.
Not so this scoured blank eye. Now, pitying

the hole's unvisited stare, I enter it
(one cell, designed), sit down. The mirror glares;
I smirk, then consider the problem
of who I'm seeking here. Read a graffito,
'Weetabix Iguana.' And my face as baffling.

Conjuring Show by Children

We practised, giggling past
our slithery fingers.
When night huddled its thick
deceptor's cloak,
we sharpened expertise,
performed our tricklets.

Guessed ourselves so damn smart,
hands slick as a lizard
who tightrope-strolls a stem,
leans tongue and cheek and
incorrupt scaly curve
to inspect some flower.

In California that night
Monroe was coaxing
a storm-frightened cow
into her livingroom.
We kids were playacting
six thousand miles from magic.

Watching Television from Bed

Feet treading the Silk Road, crusing the remorseless-
ly vacant air while commentators chat between them;
feet investigating littorals, feet limited only

by a bedrail and the calculated space beyond it.
Feet deceptive. Feet which mock the weatherman,
unlabelling zephyrs, spinning anonymous hurricanes

past his control. Feet perfect or imperfect,
supple as grammar, feet alphabetic
renewed and renewing. Feet which nudge.

Feet piggy-playing, feet uninnocent;
characterful feet which ride their leaning arches,
their calluses, like a brood mare. Feet searching

crucial yet humble; tentative feet.
Feet which seek company, feet which will turn,
luxuriant, to the other pair when TV's off;

feet silent, cold with mystery. Feet triumphant.
Feet clutching, nuzzling, coupling; feet at rest.
Feet which ban further talk of them. Loved feet. Ours.

Skeletons

In bed together our two skeletons,
one lightly sprawled on the other,
take a chatty pose, not sombre,
casual like gossip on a bus

or like the spider's web on our north wall this morning;
a thin dew showed the web lopsided,
a nearly botched work, pragmatic,
a jobbing web run up for interim use.

You move under me and, bone on bone,
we become alive. I remember the complex
city a live bone is, its cells startling as flames,
its busyness. And I recall a picture,

somewhere, of skeletons warming themselves
at an artist's stove. Our pose has broken,
our bundles of bones shift widely.
Love, hold me tight.

In the Limelight

It sounds cosy,
rounded, an invitation
most people wouldn't readily refuse.
You must read the history
of magic lanterns to discover
limelight's drawbacks: how
the word holds no hint
of the explosive mix
which the necessary gases make
(hydrogen, oxygen)
or the risk-filled imperative
of setting them alight
and directing their flame's jet
to the cylinder. No mention of
the brutish dangerous glare
from the cylinder of lime.

Instead of a Love Poem

Not enough silence here. Like air it brims our hollows
spacious and deep, but tremors run across it;
we're restless stealthers seeking to reoccupy,
by a forced entry, all the moods we've known.

Not enough space. Not voyageurs travelling the fur routes,
only two urban folk who share a takeaway
or gut each other's dreams in a lean bed
so that we wake, each morning, longing for something
tremendous.

Not enough time. Not ours the summer dusk,
the torched boat and the chanting plunge through alleys
ten centuries prolonged, the bird-scratch runic
story recurring like exotic fever.

Subtracting was the easiest – fun to cut.
Addition's tricky. The swans fly past your face
and over your prints in the salty mud as if they're quoting
some word we spoke which drained our right to silence.

Homeostasis

An extra person lives inside me, physical,
not fecund. Irritable, a pincenez person
standing at scales, weighing and sieving off
detritus. A person not interested in my thoughts

but juggling and finetuning out of a passionate love
for the skill itself, the adjusted balance which keeps
lungs at their suck and spew, heart juddering,
liver sorting its complex chemistries,

and kidneys – filter paper extraordinaire – at sifting.
A person I never see and wouldn't recognise
if opened to my gaze, a secret contriver
who mutters at me only when things go astray

and aren't fast-fixable. Then the person may lash
with cell and swarm, become a wrecker,
fling lethal moods, demolish scales and house. Normally a person
calm among riptides, jungles, an endless explorer

carrying bed and baggage and scientific
knowhow on secretive paths. A humourless person,
intense and subtle, who calculates me as algebraic
dogma, geometric progression, logic; who takes

my commands and transforms them
into curtains of light, aureoles, shifting harmonies,
swift movements, unexpected words. An interpreter
relishing the arcane. A body-person. Me.

Beach Language

The shifting figures on the beach
are mobile punctuation: comma, dot
(as – ball at play), hyphen of child
laughingly slung between its two adults.
The sun descends, shapes blur; comma and dot
slow into sharper forms, an alphabet
sparse, incorrupt, shining between
sea and wet page of beach;
an alphabet newmade
for some phonetic brand of thought.
'You want?', 'I love,' 'Happy' – these simple phrases
pass without sound among the linking letters.

Through the dusty ribbed dunes we return
from this spare and beautiful speech,
and our faces, turned to each other, my dear,
are hieroglyph, hieroglyph.

The Cockroach Century
(written in 1997)

(i)

We spread a table in the park
for someone who might return.
(Black armband, coat with three buttons)

but creatures slide out of the bushes
and squawk; they're not lives we expected.
What has tormented them?

and why does a gardener stroll
in the ruined cloister garth?
He's admiring the scene, not working;

he's disposed of all the inmates.
Soon he'll move to another country
and spade its black earth; he knows

the needed dimensions exactly,
he's dug these holes so often.

Cucumber and bread

(ancient spells) have lost their power;
during this smeared century
the cockroach is master.

Whenever you build a homestead
a wolf howls down the flue
and someone outside calls to him,

'Have a care. Softly!'
So there are refinements
of fang and claw? welcome

to the years of micro-torture.

(ii)
As inexplicably as small ponds fill and drain
in the season of dense rain
or as a mirage of curds and honey

may ripen in the desert
or as an owl ignores you on a hedge in daylight
or as that smash-hit movie of the Fifties

(tranquilly titled 'Vertigo')
can remove you from yourself into a spiral
of hissing shadows – so, a billion times more so,

this century's a masked man leaping.
Domaine perdue . . . the icy northern pinewoods
and a face at a window, flattening, gone.

The locks are broken and the river drips
like candles nailed on redhot stones; compassion
is tiredness there's no time or luxury for,

a tiredness almost native to our bones –
not some jazzed virus which the body seizes
avid for newer pains. Here's the inopportune

time, years of hallucination
induced by too much truth drug. Fragments and ruins

and only us stub-fingered to sort out

what scaffolding's required. Moreover, metal bolts
are dangerous, they can conduct
lightning. I offer you

at the edge of the raw next century, a view –
one anchorite's squinthole.
Stripped apse, a cloudy night

and a recurrent flicker which suggests that rocks
are exploding beyond the horizon,
rocks full of people. Pray for that DNA.

The Unquiet Soul

'God hath sent me to sea for pearls.' Christopher Smart

The owl and porcupine, the hawk and raven
nest on my outcroppings – but centrally
I am myself and also travelling Other,
painted stone griffin, fibrous beginning,
struggle and inequality, a place
of bandages and cradles. Some of my glasswork
is window, some mirror. The ratio is important.

A flute may cram you full of other gods,
or torn clouds alter to bizarre alphabets
and all our watches warp. This is expected.
Much stronger are the queries of knife and cloak,
a laugh or scowl of grief, the broken columns
and severed arch alongside which
Death rides us to an advertised event

and the posters are flaking before we arrive.
Therefore I've been a thief and carver and am now
battered ship's crew diving for pearls
beyond horizons. Tonight the moon hung so sharp
I could have sketched her craters, but no pearls
have yet been raised. And I cannot forget
the land left behind, the granaries of those mountains.

Composing Music

This texture precludes that. For music you must start
from a different premise, an arc less vulnerable
than words which are our rubbed and shabby purse.
In a special silence you jump, leave ground, connect
with some invisible line which borrows a curve
you didn't expect, into a place which no one
has first explored, an open land, a fearing.
A land of battling colours, vegetations.

If asked to compare these wanderings
with solid walls or murmurs, I would say,
'This is another sort of language –
as when abroad you hear, not understanding.
The gestures differ too: a nodded head
means No, a beckon Go Away.
I would say this but not have caught the edge
of the ravelling difficult thread which music is.

So music's neither language nor a thread.
Dispersed as soon as spun, and yet remaining,
it resembles certain foods, or inkwells
(the oldfashioned tubs which always spilled);
there's a comparison too with travel,
the indigenous sort where you roam sandhills,
pick grasses, chew and spit, where everything is tasted.
Music loiters and goes, is lost and arriving.

To write music is to voyage in a country
where rollercoasters are the only means of transport
(except wings, which might – although too rarely – happen),
a sky full of hawks and spiders, a supposing
that the lover's body lies alongside yours
passionate or hating, that you've slept together
for years and always will. (But in reality
you have forgotten who the lover was).

It's set down now. Indefinite questioning
is what the notes of the score no doubt resemble
to a world without pitch. We shall destroy that music,
mangle, in our attempts to make it perfect,
to give definitive performance – which is bare
crudity compared to the composer's aim.
'The Old Men of the Shells': a bagpipes keening.
At our shells we listen, shake and blow them, sing – and fail.

Restless Elegy

'Marble statues stand and look at me.' Goethe.

When I think of love and you, I see a marble surface
scored with innumerable narrow lines under a thin dust
and something is trying to break from the marble – a dilemma
wrenched on itself, of furious hope and fear.

I was no softer (two marble surfaces meeting)
but, since I lived and you died, my brittle past falters.
Meanwhile you stand dead in the bare hallway
of an echoing villa closed to rain, wind, sun,

where you work ceaselessly at dissolving the strictures,
contours, you'd learned to impose. The air in the hallway
is still, dank, makes me shiver... but I must flee in through cracks
around the monumental door to find you

and explain, accuse, shift the dust, run a loving finger
along those lines your passion scored, to ask the marble
(my live face pressing your death), 'Was hat man dir, du armes...'*
no use; we both know each was enemy,

each victim, sorcerer, each adorer. I clutch your face
and explain that the villa garden holds an orange-tree –
not the sour lemon – and there's a wide lake view, the sun...
but your cold marble says, 'What use is that to me?'

Yet – pressing you, impelled – I begin to feel your body feeding
(while memory alters like the weathers outside this shuttered place),
changing yourself and me, masticating the pair of us
to become a new couple, neither of us wholly dead

nor ordinarily alive. Your dying words at least
were fiery, unmistakable, changed the whole brew
to something so explosive that I wonder you can stand there
silent, even though busy. This chemistry which works us –

glissades the marble atoms off you like fresh sweat and sends
my own oxygenated lusts and dreads to meet them –
makes linkages not found in books, mutates our random
fumble of atoms to a fact which is not flesh or marble.

These links I hug ferociously against the coming time
when villa, lake and you are gone, the world is raw
chalcedony or salt, a train blurs the horizon
and statues, unresponsive, are dishevelled into junkyards.

* 'What has man done to you, poor child?'

Child on Bus

Shaved head, a brass chain bracelet, glitter eyes,
aged nine at most, he rides the city buses
all evening, never pays or sits.
The drivers shrug, 'Safer than on the streets.'
There's an equation here
loose-centred; he's a proposition fleeing
and I've not force to anchor.
My instinct is, to nudge him
along those passageways where women brood
ready to nurture, but they wouldn't fit
with his stance of guarding a transmission tower
deep inside enemy land. Okay, I want
to suppose I understand him sharper than
the other passengers may. (A mean-streets amble;
we're a set of scarred bonfire implements,
toastingfork, poker, charred corkscrew, several logs).

I'd inject into his head gold, silver,
silk, apes and peacocks, hand him the deeds
to the sanctuary of unicorns, pile those differing hopes
which stroll a feastday mackerel on a string. Somewhere there's surely
a world of vine stems which would suit him.

But the messy fluidness of adults
faced with spare children, and my lack of legal tender
fog me and bind.   Nameless, he leaps to transfer
and options which leaned casual now yell
like watchers at a no-holds-barred disaster.

Street king or victim, he's gone – and anyway
is neatly clothed, is fed. 'He's his own person.'
Ah, that's the problem; he's illegal young
and we're illegal about him. Startled, confused, I squint

to the dark bus stop and I wish him
safety, plus more joy than he'll maybe get.
My bleak imagination dents his future
but tries to rate it higher than a dream
in the kid's narrow skull, one midnight, when he lies
taut in a thin bed and across his face
from the bare window there slides the defiant
glory of the lit milkfloat, a patrol craft
which stopped delivering here five years ago.

China Rain

We spent a halfhour learning china rain
not cloud-seeding but hanging pottery mugs,
choosing their thickness, size, the metal rod's sharp deference,
so when you close your eyes the rain falls convincing.

There's a simplicity to this which shakes like sadness,
like the uterine curve of a sugar pig or the moment
when your child, waiting the tooth fairy, turns to search
and for the first time ever you're the phrase

he doesn't bother to listen to, the touch
he doesn't notice to replay. The going-rate
under his pillow mutates from your secret
and untaught china rain will shape his future.

Making Sugar Sculptures

In my kitchen we're making hippocampi,
those passionate sugar-horses of the mind.
Powdered sweetening, gum tragacanth
and an eighteenth-century mould which may have witnessed
the French queen's beheading. Our new horses
toss into the old shapes' lively mane,
prancing front legs, curved wings, spread scaly tail.
Stablemates of delight, now resurrected.

Between the wood mould and that guillotine
moves this centuries-lost survival, delicate
its charming fragile world. We shape the steeds
cautious and sober, crudely aware
against the bloodied background of their past
that even one teardrop would dissolve and wreck them.

Shoe Leather

'Sea leather,' says the boy,
pictures me boats as shoes walking
tainting this green repository of bodies,
spume, broken masts and a few fish

while the small islands cluster like grapeshot,
the continents oafish. Shoes walking
so many voyages, heels flapping,
sleeping rough, propositioning anonymous feet.

These scuffed shoes move like a language
on the edge of extinction, muttering
or asking. The sea yawns and a conundrum
slips its banana skin under each keel.

The First Daguerrotype

Viewed from a room shaped neatly, like a vase
overlooking this street where even the leaves tilt drunken
and the photographer's plate was necessarily exposed
so long that the crowding carriages and people
continually whiten to blankness. Only a bootblack,
spectrally crouching, remains; everyone else is
travelling too fast to be visible.

The street smelled maybe of September trees,
of apples and roast chestnuts; certainly it smelled
of horse turds, sweat and perfume. World's hot stink –
but with ungodly innocence this new invention
has already learned how to airbrush us
cleanly away from our lives. The camera's
rockinghorse eye finds no distortion

in this crude absence. But those blanks of the picture
reach back beyond camera, beyond oozy metaphor,
past the witch in the henhouse, the gingerbread foolery, the cave
of raw smoke and the hunt; they're huge gaps
before the gone mammoths strolled, gaps which keep hauling
us into before-air. As if the bootblack
is portent not history, is our charred reaching forward.

For a Child Killed by its Mother

(i)
Small legate to an unimagined land,
I dare disturb you, because no one else
has closer right. Your mother ran ahead,
your father long since melted from his duties;
remains the gaggling world you left, and me.

That morning's photo stares out cheery,
alert, as if the woman's smile discusses
only the trees, her lawn, a sunny day.
A smile peaceful as milk, certainly kindly;
you'd guess she loves. Across what frightful acres

did she trudge then to find Death sprawled indoors
fumbling himself, while from his scorched surrounding
meadows a thin smoke trailed? How did she recognise
his shack as home, his chiming watch as pager?
and why's the world still branded by her deed?

(ii)
I've staked this claim in you,
hammered at fenceposts,
raised a cabin,
installed live heat and
birthed, in the half-loft,
my intrusive sorrow.

But I lived in London
that winter too,
your mother and I
both shifting, unpacking,
puzzled at plumbing,
new curtains, woodworm.

We could have met,
coincided, befriended.
Between us, dead child,
we might have saved you.

(iii)
howl next because I have no kids
rather break rocks on the mountain road
smash open other private lives like yours
to feed this absence

salt hard biscuit on the world's tongue
net drawn up dripping glittering bare of fish
I imprison myself in a nest of spangles to mourn
that future's absence

then angled on some stream delicately leaning
my bait plunges through the clear towards you
or other person yet unknown yet hunted
in fear of absence

from inside a clock I talk now its hammers striking
around me the Perspex face veers in shame while I shameless
proclaim a moratorium on decent grieving
I'll rob your absence

(iv)
You monstrous fish
'all seasnakes are venomous'
you writhe smash all apart
in the whirl of your tail.

A green-ice winter
cupped in the house unplungeable
frostheads gawped the windows
trigonometric leaks the floor.

Winter to strain
sanity like string tugged
mine creaked hers broke
odds you can't calculate.

To work and from
sleeping scrubbing eating
all our compassions frozen
ice-ages under.

(v)
The flick of feathers on the sky
is world's least noise, partway
between sound and non, a query
at the cusp of the air.

Next the embalmer's art
swims in the jar; there's a distortion.
Peaceful in formalin
eyes crease, the baby smiles.

Let's move a halo from another sequence
and plant it here; the looped gold wire
circles a flippant veil, twin castles,
many short rounded hills.

She carries seed-pearls on her head, as you,
infant, a circle at your throat.
Smile in the fluid where we cannot help you;
now, grey-rimmed preacher, crease your eyes and grin.

(vi)
Yes, your dad lives,
re-wed, sired more kids,

swims in the summer river,
fucks her under the moon.

He and your mother
had split, as couples may;

some said she'd pressed him,
some – he ran loose.

The why's in the ground now
and in his head.

Wet muscles glisten.
What do I want – his drowning?

(vii)
People talk differently at night.
Auden, speaking in Italy,
requested guilt and received gold leaf;

guilt is reserved for murder.

Velvet, this season's chic fabric,
slides midnight-dark across our options
on to the bridge which will fall if we do not
break stride, loosen our rush.

Chaos theory: random processes
prove logical if long enough continued.
All adults fight; where's the construction
will wrestle logic from that punching fact?

I and the world can offer this infant
only sleep, with which his bones are glutted.
If I could have stolen him – honesty breaks down,
wraps itself in velvet, flees. Despise me.

The Friendship of Mansfield and Woolf

Two skittery birds in a dance
part war, part courtship, and all ritual.

Their mutual love of writing
surges like water over coin-shaped shingle.

A perfect arrow or an infant's finger . . .
there are no words, no words. The mind sweats and coughs

or shivers like a hawk at an abyss;
this is what it means to be working.

So these two stand, with their drawn wings
for weapons, each woman breasting her private terror

but they talk, they discuss the acts of the mind
fluently, passionate, while Murry oozes thick motor oil

and the sky rains comet-tails not tears.
They harness moths to measure nerve reactions

while sheet-headed night gathers outside their window
and men deliver coal and on the fountain

ice flexes or dies. At home Leonard worries,
"She'll tire herself." Eighty years after,

I glimpse a photograph of women trying
to pitch a tent before the sandstorms hit them.

'Lorenz' and Other Codes

A code with a duelling-scar on its cheek and a field-grey cloak,
Lorenz. And others. Are they good at their job,
these lean pale whippet types? Superb.
Worker-mutes bang with small hammers
and twiddle rotor arms to spew the codes,
but foreign interceptors grab
and masticate them like a disease
intensive, stealing.

                    The machines have names:
Enigma, Colossus, Purple – as playground kids might yell a taunt
and the teacher mutters, 'Maybe it will all end
peaceably.' Then the greyhounds, baulked
of chasing the mad moustachio'd hare,
will whine into the mist and only the dead men,
with straw in their mouths, rise puzzled.

Seahenge

A beach: twentyfirst century. The North Sea fidgets
round upturned oak tree and a rotting circle
of logs on end. We roughly guess
at what this tribe believed: how the dead soul,
cradled in roots and stunned by air, is sucked
down through the trunk, the branches, to deep sand
and plays there, flings, disperses,
till its constituent hopes like chemicals go travelling,
break up and link with other hopes assured
in that wet silicate next-world. Hearts of live mourners
rasp but accept, are damaged pottery.
                    Everything's yet to come
which we call world, yet theirs is full, enclosed;
within their rite they don't need us.
We're crude, unthinkable.

Streptococcal Infection of the Heart

Gold is formed by the clashing of two stars.
And something clashed in my heart, a rare metal
struck from the bite of strep on endothelium.
Three days before,
walking that coastal town, I'd seen a shop
selling only species of door;
the tarry air fed silent through each gape.

'Can I listen to your heart?'
Not noticeably. Not unless you must.
He bends, he frowns, the stethoscope clings cold.
After he's gone
I try to read. Norse story,
'In an eclipse a wolf eats up the sun.'
Leaning, leaning at the core of this mystery

sneers the untiring wolf; its breath
strikes the world with a sense of something tremendous
ready to open out.
Through the cosmos's head
(to stalemates only, rustbucket wars)
lovers of Bach and Elgar trundle bombloads;
the earth and I are travelling stalks of fire –

but I long to yell how personal this is,
how the combat's entirely between the wolf and me,
no one else present. Twenty bread-mould pills,
that's all the help.

My body (toughish, not entirely young)
fights the wolf who's incredibly ancient yet sharp
barnacled with malice, charm, cunning.

It's over, he's gone – somewhere. To a cave
or dungeon to chew at his wounds and replan?
The battle scarred us both. A narrow personal fight?
Surely, like fractious servants,
all the emotions now alive on earth cry No
while they watch, from their warm caging basement,
his raw flanks in the quaintly patterned snow.

Learning Russian

A language like a ploughshare
and the clods gleam metallic,
each falling aside with the exact shimmer
of blue steel under an Arctic sun.
I hunt the page and a glimmer
descends here, nowhere, from the glowworm
which squats upon my wrist, white grublike
remnant of ancient curiosity.

First phrase translates: Here house.
Much is left out, is assumed,
and word-stress, though important,
is rarely what we expected.
The place-names shiver and become other
like branches reflected in turbulent water;
so Moscow is a yawn with a thump at its end
and never an 'o' to the sound.

Language to describe fermented milk, museums,
snowy streets, Vogue and coarse betrayals,
birch woods and extinct mammoths
and 'I-cannot-sleep-till-I-know-you-sleep' soul-sharing
and wooden watchtowers rotting on the frontier.
And, in Kolyma, the language
of rack upon rack, brown folders of dead men
who rise and speak now that the sun is shining.

The letters of Cyrillic look like gates,
like flowers opening or like small explosions
controlled from elsewhere, or old women
gathering mushrooms in contaminated forests;
dense squiggles on a battered seismograph.
Your breathing gets altered, and metre
(that heartbeat) shoves itself remorseless.
Your tongue is sent on baffling corkscrew journeys.

An English poem that's translated
and then translated back, returns crammed
with a tough vividness. The abstractions
have gone away like pale birds
blown on a mist; the verbs
have speeded up and the nouns –
solid as bread, rich as caviare – march.
There is a vast country somewhere, singing.

Osip Mandelshtam

Paper is lethal. A cold dangerous breath
fidgets the door. On many nights his skin
contains the wrong body. After his arrest
imagine a desert where no images exist,
not even the image of sand.

In wooden watchtowers the guards
aim rifles for their ancient sport
to the young snow and birch trees. He does not
live long. After his death his Gulag file
is labelled, 'To be kept for ever.'

The bruised forest waited, the short poems he'd made –
comet-sparks in that desert, obstinate agate-and-gold,
swan-bite when all swans had been debeaked –
stayed hidden in friends' rote-learning until,
thirty years late, the ringbarked trees began
inevitable movement of their fibres.

Girl with Daffodil

Exact as a head on a coin
she regards the daffodil, which in turn
regards her. Drenching waves of emotion –
her companions' and mine – break round her night-ringed face
but she's not there. She is all daffodil.

The wet pavement, drunken shouts, thick dark...
She says, 'I want to see him again,' but her lust
is smothered, neutered, by the daffodil
to a gilt peace, a slight delicate scent.
A passing man catches my eye and I'm raw

while the girl still gazes into the yellow secret
as if those pistils, stamens, are her mind, a curled gold thought.
No thorns there and no smirr of greasy road;
these chewing-gum details have all dropped away,
her skimped black dress, her rakish hair, even her words.

At last along the trumpet she slowly falters,
draws herself back towards the world like a person wounded.
She smiles, says, 'Do you think he'll come soon?' but muted,
voice stumbling, weighted like the daffodil. Then finally outside,
inside herself, she smiles deep, breathes, lets the tired flower lie.

The Small Green Elephant

'Moi-même, que je hais comme une épouse.' Valéry.
'Yeats... happened to observe that an acquaintance was followed
by "a small green elephant. And then," the poet added, "I knew he
was a very wicked man." ' Ellman.

In honeycomb armour I walk the town,
at home I turn and face myself this spouse.
Daywatchman, public warden, be assured
your doubts of me are not original.

Myself inspects myself from constant habit,
cautions and warns unanswered. I'm
a small green elephant who follows myself,
not as sour omen but investigates,
mistrust, critiques. We two are creatures
from the bizarrest circus of the world,
human and shadowing-human self.

Here's a relationship past family trees;
married? perhaps. Who's explored spousal hate?
Crosslatch all fingers like an infant's steeple
and swear fidelity, but dust-years slither through.

I've hated a lover who died too young;
what jungle beasts has that earned? My salt man
drank the warm waves; I can't reach him to punish.
Sometimes I've hated being loved
because the lover loved a greygreen shadow
which walked ahead. I couldn't glimpse its face.

This northern street's sheltered by jacarandas;
this house, gush satin. In front of my plodding feet
the creature drops its various reeking turds
and I inspect them. Strange sour bloodied creature!
Yet my dismay and ridicule fuse to a shifty passion,
corrupted love. I'll guard the creature's secrets.

Reading Detective Stories

These bare or psychotic excitements –
the bald financier in his library
or stink of bitter almonds in the cellar
or figure armed and leaning at the window –
distil themselves from crudely flung collages
(wrecked news clippings and smears of gossip)
into a blind yet strong necessity
which holds, manipulates, weaves its own logic.

Each story builds a pyramid in the brain;
museums glitter off it; casual people –
hooded or cowled or naked, mute or muttering –
walk at the corners of our narrow sight.
They're all important. This is the one ethical
and purest artform, honed like an equation
but bringing in that alien huge dimension:
bell and cart in the street, a chalked cross on the door.

The grammar of humanity keeps us silent,
absorbed by footwork's deftness and a villain
we live inside. The Golden Age books
were chess; now we're more complex, brutal,
wistful detective tangling with subtle murderer,
no simple answers. Only the reach of soul,
unsought removal men backing and filling –
and then the charnel, leaving us satisfied.

The Automaton

Woman with scarlet dress, dark hair,
gold rod in your hand, plush table
before you with three covered platters,
your bold stare offers fears
brilliant as a paintbox; I leap in.

The mechanism creaks; if I dared touch you
a drop of oil would help, but I don't dare,
your exactness scares me. Now you tap a platter,
first lightly then imperious; the gilt lid rises.
Small ivory skull. Why should I feel surprised?

Your rictus grin. (Automata don't smile
but you've acquired this human habit
as humans could acquire a car or shoes).
The skull smiles too. Who made you, scarlet monster?
what cave of goblins pulled the strings in him?

She raises her gold rod, considers,
then taps the second cover. A pig's snout.
Three grins now: hers, the bored skull's grin, the offal's.
(Outside, flittering June rain smirrs the window).
Next, her smile deepens, leaves the rest behind,

warms to near-friendly – but her smile stays bold,
triumphant; she knows what we don't.
She lifts the rod and poises it, then starts to tap
the third gilt cover. Terror has filled the room,
no space for breath or grin, only for terror.

What mind devised her, and in what torment?
Whatever price the saleroom put on her would falter
and shrivel; she's all collectors' lust.
But she taps the third lid, grins that knowing smile,
rictus of agony; silently she's transformed

while the lid rises... No, she mustn't live.
I fling myself upon her; there's a clatter,
old metal, bits of rusty dress, surround me;
I'm led shambling away. A price is named –
as if she were like other toys and one could barter

pure sorrow for pure need. I pay the price
(with her, all usual coinage is derisory),
blow her dust from my hands, scrub off her scent,
shudder away the fragments of skulll and snout.
Who made this evil thing? Slowly my own self answers.

Nudity

The air does ridiculous things to naked crevices;
walking a beach, I can testify. Those effects flood through
to torment my mind with a storm of pleasure. But I am not
Picasso's Chameleon (discovered two years ago
and retro-named) which ridged and bulked creature
invents spectra according to mood
but can also lick its own eyes. I cannot lick
even an extensive part of myself: the eye
is quite out of bounds. I want a significant other
and closer than the air, to lick my eyes. Yesterday

someone spoke about wildcats, how the manul
has blunt ears and a fuzzed grey coat
to help it stay hidden. I am not a manul
whose aqueous stare hits much stranger
than this walked-on watery horizon. I shall never
understand the manul. But a chameleon
might understand me rather closely,
near enough, at least, to disconcert. I was stared at once
by a salamander; neither of us has forgotten.
Since then the air strokes with astonishing promises.

The Arrivers

The people who hang on hooks behind the door,
the nighttime folk, wide-shouldered, cloaked,
ready to leap down and get personal:
surely you've met them too.

The face-which-isn't-a-face is most scary,
a gape within the shirt collar, an affront
soundless, invisible. You hope that when you grow up
you won't see them any more. Believe me,

they come differently. Instead of silence they mutter,
instead of leaping, fumble. The reassuring times
are when they briefly jump at you full-throated
as in your youth. Then you could almost love them.

Prime Numbers

Darkset against the sky (their secrets
buried beneath them, as stone menhirs)
they rise from the underbrush of ordinary numbers.

Those other numbers are profligate, rioting
in swift divisions and a fevered riddling;
these stand aloof in intermittent grouping.

Poke at their pasts and you will not discover
any acquisitive trick of friend or lover;
no simple cross or piling pyramid connects one to another.

And play such spatial war-games as you will,
these are invaders you cannot repel;
they are core-solid, indestructible.

The other numbers – formed like mercury from droplets –
impassioned, run and pleat like messy humans;
we recognise their urges and fecundities.

Prime numbers are as alien as moondust,
sterile, desireless, an astonishment,
unease and inexplicable. Their sole fact: they exist.

Towing an Iceberg

The white cat trudges up the garden.
White cats have a reputation, yet she
is neither deaf nor blind.
But she is a ghost.

She enters this house, towing
the weight of the loss of her into my heart;
she is a police launch towing an iceberg
clear of familiar shipping lanes.

'When she arrives at your door
open it at once or she will die,'
(instruction from a necromancy manual).
Too late: the cat now surrounds me,
she is white as a unicorn with disaster
and the weight of the iceberg most terrible to her;
in cat-speak she tells me so.

The dimensions of her are small but the concept
huge beyond knowing; she contains
multitudes who stagger and faint.
Her gaze confesses all.

She jumps to the forbidden peacock-chair,
sorts her body, limbs, tail, becomes ice.
The sun gleams on a thread of cane, the chairback
curved above vacant seat, puzzled air.

Old

Not cooling with age but incandescent,
hospital bed steered by a reckless driver
slamming into legs, breaking hearts. Indelicate profferer
of unwanted advice; tireless seeker
of the child mislaid so many years ago.
The old gather up their reins
to hunt, deflect. Protect yourself from them.

Yet I've seen a smile, wide, benignant,
on those scoured faces when it's least expected.
She's dead now, carrying her smile with her –
a trophy – to the land of wrecked cornfields
and ease; giving us up. Far through the trees
comes tinny music from the carousel, and a floodmark
glowers high above us.

But her smile's floodmark too. So we
(suddenly abandoned beside the river)
provisionally born, provisionally soon to die,
burn with the fire of gods or each other. Never suppose
we can't tremble with disastrous happiness
till our last moment. See, my hand shakes
even now with love for a man, under the floodmark.

Questions

Small children ask at slantwise to the world,
they're new spring froglets shrilling our bare creek
with a dazzle of code. From them I've learned
to recognise the unhappiness of fireplugs,
the inch-tall men dancing a rain-drenched sidewalk,
the pitiful frailty of an ounce of gin.

Someday we'll teach them solid manifestations:
the lure of ancient starlight caught in jamjars,
or how a piece of scrimshaw is the whale
or, in some trendy baker's shop,
Gingerbread Persons aren't quite anatomic.
But toddlers are out of reach, they always were.

Not with a set prenatal radiance but simply
they ask at us from places which didn't exist
until these infants found them. Kids can be brusque
and savage, but their different logic
opens the dark-and-light beyonds to them,
brings freedom of all their thought, no limit.

The moons in my pocket shiver like a stallion:
future moons, money moons, moons of hard passion
ready to weight this child. I long to hold him
back from their loop, preserve his startling self.
No use. My wish is as naive as him
and as impossible to bind. Already

I start to see how he becomes
reasonable – a slight inconsequent dulling
which builds on his thirst, his increased knowledge;
a closure of diamond possibilities.
Those whetsome-moons have laid their smear of dust
and continue to spin round him. Child – boy – adult.

The Boy in the Thorn Tree

Not schoolchildren perched over their textbooks,
groomed, lively, nor the heft of years
caught in a tidy balance between them and me –
but the extra child, the one whose logic was speared
by shadows which use dynamite to stun their prey
then toss it out of water to become merely
a cry in some thorn tree.

I mean he, terrified of school, now sees
himself a subject for debate
and – angry at self but medics too – slides tighter
impaled upon these thorns. The dews evaluate
his young blood; nights are years; strange syrups question him,
cold linctus hurts or tries to heal. Braw fighter,
desperate new loser

shrunken from fasting and resilient only
against our terracotta stare,
he now – suspended in branches – hears intently
the tumult of his illness. Nothing other
except when fragments of past learning, needle-sharp,
slide at him like those thorns. Our world stands silently
attempting, patiently.

Useless to chase the hubbub, for it wrecks,
distorts, deafens. Soon, we hope,
the medicines of inorganic chemistry
will soften thorns and terror and, with expert guile,

draw him out, bandage. The future's huge, fogged, wide,
but I beg that, whatever, he'll never again be
a cry in some thorn tree.

Form SSA-7162-OCR-SM

Item 6 refers to the child
you may not be living with now.
Place an X in the box

and say when the child left. (Do not
give a reason, do not express
emotion; simply insert

a date). In the next space
say when the child returned. If the child
has not returned, enter

'Not Returned'. (Do not attempt
to apportion blame; no excuse
will be regarded as adequate

from either party). Next, enter
the name of the child who did not return to you.
(If you and your wife disagreed,

at the christening, about choice of name,
insert both versions. But do not
make personal remarks about your wife:

there are severe penalties
for defacing this form).
In the next box you may now

insert child's reason for leaving. (Do not
overburden with detail. But if
you say, 'Violence,' 'Drugs' or 'Kidnap'

we may possibly wish to learn more.
Do not try to excuse
whatever your conduct was).

Finally, the child's present address.
(What do you mean, 'Don't Know'?
You're its father, aren't you?

Facetiousness, tears, agony
or rage will not be tolerated:
the form has no space for them.
Your grief is not a credible option).

Skidbladnir

The ship of the Norse gods; legend says
it could be folded up
and slipped into your pocket
where it would snarl
and thresh its ribbed sails
and weep, as all myths do,
and you would try to comfort it.

Gods in your pocket, tiny souls
who lash out at each other in the spiral rigging
and clutch thin ropes which are ready to dissolve.
These gods sob almost like humans in your pocket
while they watch Asgard crumble beneath them,
its gape of death under the ruined keel.

Yet they remember that this their flinty religion
commands them to die bravely, upright, bold.
The commotion in your pocket quiets down, they chant
of the sword in the bed, the circle of fire, the incest.
Then their bladderwrack begins to rot, the hull
breaks apart; soon nothing remains
except the reek of salt and a fierce wetness.
But don't assume you are freed from those small gods: their tears
are your own tears, you are made of salt water.

LIGHT VERSE

'The Times' Bicentenary

(with thanks to Sir John Betjeman)

Tea on the lawn for Joan and me
'mid prescient far-off chimes,
 with scones and honey, lace cloth, nerves
 and bicentennial 'Times.'

'Of course you take it? Daddy says –'
 O praise so comprehensive!
 Dear alto lauding fashion, sport,
 dear journal, Joan-extensive!

'If they stopped publishing – ' appalled.
'Yes, wouldn't that be rotten?'
 Beneath the lace, knees coincide;
 the Thunderer drops forgotten.

Role Switching

How do I love you, wife? let's count the ways.
I love your early-morning rush from house
trailing o.j., bran flakes and full briefcase;
I love your murderous scorn of straying mouse;
I love to think of you in hard-topped hat
trudging, absorbed and brisk, your building sites,
or costing up with frown your yards and tonnes
or balancing your books on summer nights;
I love the faded jeans your leisure wears
and man-size shirt (I'd gladly lend them all),
the conference phone that decorates your bed
the telexes which drift around our hall;
these touches send my quivering psyche wild.
But, most of all, I long to bear your child.

Treasure-trove

(On a hoard of Roman coins dug up in a field)

'But where did you hide them, Julius?
What do you mean – 'Don't know'?
You buried the blasted coins and said
we'd dig them when Nero the Emp was dead.
Now the old man's croaked and you're trying to say
you've forgotten the place, the amount, the day.
You'd better remember, Jule –
or else.

Trouble is, when we find and dig them
and get them into circ,
we'll have missed the highest interest rate
and it's hell of a lot of work.
So brisk up your tired grey matter
and cut the evasive patter
or they'll be lost for ages, Jule.'
They were.

Term of Endearment

'Why do Frenchwomen address their husbands fondly as "mon petit chou?"
Cabbage is a dull and malodorous vegetable.' (Letter to 'The Times')

A cabbage is a lovesome thing
God wot,
firm flesh
no rot;
for slaw or pickle
a lovely ickle
hard-bouncing bod
a greeny god
refulgent sliced
magnetic spiced.
So keep your sugared Valentine,
I'm very sure the cabbage must be mine.

EARLY POEMS

Delphi

There is in you that kind of arrogance the Delphic boy,
gathering the harsh reins in his unseared hand,
flung out upon the world, and now endures
carved sharp in metal, as the lunar loneliness
erodes your eyes, your lips, and fragment landscapes
glitter within your hair.

You should not be
caught up in cities, but on some white hill
above a sun-baked sea
gather your reins, while death shrinks back uncertain
to his bleak cavern on the Delphi heights
as your swift breath drives on the ghostly team.

Your face is pitiless to me, to others gentle,
but always in the echoes of your voice that boy
leaps to huzzah his team upon some stony hillside,
to count the world well-lost while he spurs onward,
while the great thighs of his dead horses gather
and underfoot ebbs up the broken thyme.

1963

'We Lay Together'

We lay together,
the man and I. Soon his bare arm
moved warm upon my own bare flesh.
He leaned across and clicked the lamp, smiled in the darkness.
His hands strayed on me, 'Happy?' I stirred and muttered,
then pulled him close. He seemed quite satisfied.
'Put out the light and then put out the light.'

After, we lay in dark
and casual talked, at length fell silent;
quite soon he slept. I listened to his breathing,
this kind good man who has no ties to me,
does not love me and whom I do not love,
no meeting save the flush of sensual pleasure...
And, still awake, I thought how strange it is

that he should wander thus,
this smiling stranger should possess my body
while you, to whom I should lie wholly open –
soul, flesh, emotions, have been yours for ever
and always will – you want no part of me,
this Spring-caught land not know your hot sun's rising:
'Put out the light and then put out the light.'

1983

Mother/child

Of this most intricate and sharp relation
nothing remains except the last faint twitching of the puppet
which in your lifetime never danced to please you,
whirling on every path except the soft and tender,
and now jerks dying in a futile effort
to love you, to conform.

Perhaps it would not greatly trouble you that, musing,
I am not certain what we felt for one another:
a child half-changeling in its fierce detachment
and you flame-searching but incapable of comfort,
of that warm easy flooding reassurance
which other parents, other children, know.

I can share the conventional feelings only when twilight
(the poet's stock-in-trade) or a birdsong overtake me
or when woodsmoke catches the throat and suddenly,
as the blue shadow lifts toward the sky, my eyelids dazzle
and I know that I have forgotten the deep significance
of that song or that pool.

My mother walks beside the bending willow;
a thousand Ophelias glitter through her hair.
She goes so softly that the blackbird, singing
in gentle undertone of love and madness,
does not remark her between flute and trumpet
nor see her foot upon the uncrushed grass.

In life we never walked those fields together
but now – she dead, I absent – we go smiling
(or is it only she who smiles?) beneath the willow,
trouble the unbrushed dew, or pull a switchet
half from the hedge and let it spring back noiseless
to join the noiseless brambles in their watch.

The owls will fly about us but we uncaring,
exploring the deep woods of each other's heart,
go where neither moonlight nor the coming dawn shall touch us,
where the pale sweeps of Norfolk glimmer in the shadows
and the rose hangs on the porch through some more heady twilight,
some spectral June.

I forgot – it is your body that feeds the rose tree.
The wind blows bitter and in sudden flurry
knifed leaves whirl down upon the moonlit arbours
where I walk with a ghost; knifed leaves, and the world disintegrates,
the road rings out in harshness and is pavements,
the clean air soots, I urban wake alone.

The blackbird sings from the low suburban rooftop
in this, as in all other, chill March days,
and while his gentle voice retells of love and murder
I walk, past the springing rose, in streets that prefigure summer
while the ghostly leaf-fall erodes my fine pretensions
and the ultimate icy air congeals the twitching doll.

The strings lie spent, the wood limbs gathering cobwebs,
the pale wood face stares out aloof at the empty
wide rows of seats where once an audience shouted,
sang, whistled, catcalled... and now rats run softly.
Here is our stage; here, played, our tiny drama.
I am a coin whose sharp obverse is dead.

1962

Loss of a Vocation to the Priesthood

Suddenly night – and Carolina waves
beat on my deviant ears with regimented roar.
I walk the darkening beach, the boardwalk flanking,
a row of ill-assorted hotel fronts, the shore,
while Carolina wind
gusts through the webbing crannies of my brain
and Carolina wrack and foam
drift at my feet where the spent tide-surge tarries,
till I have urgently a strange and sharp
presentiment of coming home.

I wrestle on this beach hour after hour
but do not find the enemy I hoped to fight,
and when I turn to face Him only the empty
darkness sighs misting in my thought. O sudden night!
Nox beatissima!
'O night that broughtest us lover to Love –'
It checks, the rhythm cannot hold;
in stumbling vers libre that I thought a sonnet
I suffer now the great emancipation,
flung naked on Orion's liquid gold.

I remember hearing the Bishop's voice,
neat, small and cautious, chiselling the silences,
breaking down personality, exploring the gulf,
the 'all for love' behind his clergy's reticences.
No doubt we did not mean
what the old playwright had in mind at all,

being men drilled in meditation
to pull up carnal wisps like green spring nettles.
We sought another love – or were we wrong?
The night wind chills my dissertation.

'You must now consider carefully,'
proclaimed the Bishop in his smiling
meticulous small voice – oh savage smiling,
oh meaningless small gesture of distressing –
'now calmly bring to mind
what time you have been given, absence sought
and gladly granted, but I must
ask soon for your decision. You have answered
with compromise before. We can no longer – '
Looking at him, I see the dust

fall sifting on his eyes, his brain, his slight
small voice that musicks on my painful heart
(or what I felt with: God knows there was something).
I said, 'Perhaps the Church and I should live apart.'
The words illjudged, a storm
rose slanting from his cautious brows and reared
tempestuous head. 'The Church – to go?
You mean to leave the Church?' Useless explaining
I have been fish-raised in her groundswell, calling
all her tides friend, all brother. 'No.'

'Then what? I will give you,' said the Bishop,
'another month, after which I shall need to hear
your final decision.' He shuffled papers,

lowered his head to them. I stood; so much unclear,
so much unspoken lay
between him and myself, like a grey ghost
that almost blocked me from the door.
He half looked up; I shoved the ghost and left.
Grey Bishop and grey ghost, I do not think
to see them or my past life any more.

But his questions buzz in my mind. 'There is
no woman in the case?' I shook my head in rage
that this should be his first and only intuition.
I should have said, 'Thousands. Take any empty page
of any old romance,
write on it what you will of fear and grief
and rage and love. My heart lies there.'
Have loved them all, from Mary with her shining
immaculate crown, to Abelard's
grieving pale nun or Macbeth's rare

and guilt-encrusted wife. And I have loved
their modern counterparts, detailing anguished choice
in dark confessional, or penance room
sit face to face, demure guilt catching at their voice,
a glowing in the eyes
as if to say, 'I tell God I regret
but still He knows that though I try
I cannot quite forget those ecstasies,
those facts which race the blood.' They muse, while on
their lips contrition slides brook-shy,

brook-smooth, and I avert my virgin thought
from the eyes' glow, the reminiscent lifting smile,
my hand up like a soldier's for the promised,
the ritual benediction. And my gaze meanwhile
rests on the ritual black
sway of my cassock, wall against temptation.
I should have said, 'I loved them all,
their hope, their desperation, their desiring.
I shared as man and priest is meant to share.
Is not the human state a call

to love, to suffer and to weep?' But I
brooding said nothing, and the Bishop guessed me
sullen, no doubt, or devious or deceiving.
'No,' I said sharply, for his question hurt me.
(Can we not watch or trust?)
'There was no technical wrongdoing here,
no plain adultery to grasp,
there is no woman.' Walking by the water
with the fall winds biting my face and old
shipwrecks giving me icy clasp,

it seems I was not honest, should have said,
'I loved, died, suffered; what were you expecting?'
I tried to live with Christ. Perhaps I did not
wholly succeed. In this is my rejecting,
deserved or no. The Christ
dying and living in me is the force
who binds me to myself and so
to the cold fall wind, the darkening night

(whether of flesh or spirit) and the wrack
the Carolina waves fling at my feet. I was a published,
a public Christ, a brand thrust up for burning.
Now I am stripped. To the secular surges of life,
a secular attempt at Christ, I go.

1982